*Pig [Swamp] Songs*

***ALSO BY***
*Abram Rooney*


**Drama**
*Where Nothing Arrives (Playdead Press)*


**Poetry**
*Empty Arrows (Mysterium)*

# *Pig [Swamp] Songs*

*Abram Rooney*

Published by Playdead Press

© Abram Rooney 2023

Abram Rooney has asserted his rights under the Copyright, Design and Patents Act, 1988, to be identified as the author of this work.

A CIP catalogue record for this book is available from the British Library.

978-1-910067-91-8

This book is sold subject to the condition that it shall not by way of trade or otherwise, be lent, resold, hired out, or otherwise circulated without the publisher's prior consent in any form of binding or cover other than that in which it is published and without a similar condition including this condition being imposed on the subsequent purchaser.

Playdead Press
www.playdeadpress.com

*Death is Not the End* © Bob Dylan, 1988, Special Rider Music
*Hugh Selwyn Mauberley [Part I]* © Ezra Pound, 1926, New Directions Publishing Corp
*Mother of Muses* © Bob Dylan, 2020, Special Rider Music
*Song of Myself,* Walt Whitman, 1892, in Public Domain

*For Kara*

*The tree of life is growing
where the spirit never dies,
and the bright light of salvation shines
in dark and empty skies.*

Bob Dylan, *Death is Not the End*

# Contents

*Introduction by Simon Usher*      i

| | |
|---|---|
| The Tree Surgeon | 3 |
| The Swamp [One] | 4 |
| The Enemy's Apples [One] | 5 |
| The Swamp [Two] | 6 |
| Interlude [One] | 7 |
| Leaf Fairies [One] | 8 |
| Leaf Fairies [Two] | 9 |
| Leaf Fairies [Three] | 10 |
| Peter [One] | 11 |
| Lucy [One] | 13 |
| Pig Song [One] | 15 |
| Interlude [Two] | 16 |
| The Enemy's Apples [Two] | 17 |
| The Swamp [Three] | 18 |
| Ma [One] | 19 |
| David [One] | 20 |
| Spiderwebs | 21 |
| Ma [Two] | 22 |
| Pig Song [Two] | 23 |
| Interlude [Three] | 24 |
| Ma [Three] | 25 |
| Counting Trees | 26 |
| Interlude [Four] | 27 |
| Lucy [Two] | 29 |
| David [Two] | 31 |
| Lucy [Three] | 32 |

| | |
|---|---:|
| Old Man | 33 |
| Lucy [Four] | 34 |
| The Enemy's Apples [Three] | 36 |
| Pig Song [Three] | 37 |
| Lucy [Five] | 38 |
| A Lake Memory | 41 |
| Water | 43 |
| Lucy [Six] | 44 |
| Ma [Four] | 46 |
| Lucy Six [Reprise] | 47 |
| Pig Song [Four] | 48 |
| Interlude [Five] | 49 |
| Lucy [Seven] | 50 |
| The People's Soul | 51 |
| Lucy [Eight] | 52 |
| Interlude [Six] | 54 |
| The Rain | 55 |
| The Enemy's Apples [Four] | 56 |
| Bird Song | 57 |
| Pig Song [Five] | 59 |
| Lucy [Nine] | 60 |
| David [Three] | 61 |
| You Trim Them Back | 62 |
| Ma [Five] | 63 |
| Interlude [Seven] | 65 |
| Pig Song [Six] | 66 |
| The Enemy's Apples [Five] | 67 |
| The Famous Red | 68 |
| Interlude [Eight] | 71 |
| David [Four] | 72 |
| Ma [Six] | 75 |

| | |
|---|---|
| Interlude [Nine] | 76 |
| Ma [Seven] | 77 |
| David [Five] | 78 |
| Lighter Now, Riding Clouds [One] | 79 |
| Lighter Now, Riding Clouds [Two] | 80 |
| Lighter Now, Riding Clouds [Three] | 81 |
| Lighter Now, Riding Clouds [Four] | 82 |
| Lighter Now, Riding Clouds [Five] | 83 |
| Lighter Now, Riding Clouds [Six] | 84 |
| Peter [One] | 85 |
| Interlude [Ten] | 86 |
| Counting Trees [Two] | 87 |
| The Enemy's Apples [Six] | 88 |
| Peter's Twin | 89 |
| Worth It | 90 |
| Gentle Forehead | 91 |
| David [Six] | 92 |
| Pebble Eyes [One] | 93 |
| David [Seven] | 94 |
| Pebble Eyes [Two] | 95 |
| David [Eight] | 96 |
| Lucy [Ten] | 97 |
| David [Nine] | 98 |
| Masses of Blood | 99 |
| David [Ten] | 100 |
| Lucy [Eleven] | 101 |
| David [Eleven] | 102 |
| Lucy [Twelve] | 103 |
| David [Twelve] | 104 |
| Lucy [Thirteen] | 105 |
| Interlude [Eleven] | 106 |

| | |
|---|---|
| The Enemy's Apples [Seven] | 107 |
| Counting Trees [Three] | 108 |
| Interlude [Twelve] | 109 |
| The Horse [One] | 110 |
| The Only Honest Thing [One] | 111 |
| The Horse [Two] | 112 |
| The Only Honest Thing [Two] | 113 |
| The Horse [Three] | 114 |
| The Enemy's Apples [Eight] | 115 |
| Counting Trees [Four] | 116 |
| An Old-Fashioned Pram | 117 |
| Pig Song [Eight] | 118 |
| Pa [Two] | 119 |
| Luce | 120 |
| Tapestry | 121 |
| David [Thirteen] | 122 |
| Lucy [Fourteen] | 123 |
| David [Fifteen] | 124 |
| Interlude [Thirteen] | 125 |
| Large Bump | 126 |
| Where'd He Come From | 127 |
| Reasons | 128 |
| David [Sixteen] | 129 |
| Peter [Two] | 130 |
| The Enemy's Apples [Nine] | 131 |
| Remembering Trees | 132 |
| Interlude [Fourteen] | 134 |
| A Tap | 135 |
| Interlude [Fifteen] | 137 |
| David [Seventeen] | 138 |
| That Night | 140 |

| | |
|---|---|
| The Enemy's Apples [Ten] | 141 |
| Lady in the City [One] | 142 |
| The Old-Fashioned Pram [Reprise] | 143 |
| Lady in the City [Two] | 144 |
| Interlude [Sixteen] | 145 |
| Counting Trees [Five] | 146 |
| Slow March | 147 |
| ★ | 149 |
| | |
| Pig Songs | 151 |

## *Introduction*

by Simon Usher

When Abram Rooney was preparing to perform an earlier draft of his song-poem *Pig [Swamp] Songs* at The Old Red Lion Theatre, London, in 2018, he asked me to help with some direction in the latter stages. I had recently been working with him on another play and found him to be an unusually intelligent and, indeed, poetic actor. Reading *Pig [Swamp] Songs* for the first time, I was struck by its fluid stanzas and raw, mysterious phrases of action. It also had a very real flavour of the countryside and country people, which Abe embodied through his rough, yearning Suffolk accent and tone. This was no conventional 'new' play. In fact, it seemed touched by early twentieth-century modernism, oddly recalling Wyndham Lewis's *Enemy of The Stars*, in which Arghol stands alone in a gesture of defiance against the elements, and, less obscurely, the sixties experiments of the Living and Open Theatres in New York, such as *The Serpent*. *Pig Songs* is a work which listens to the world, without striving neurotically after character and plot. It eludes definition.

> All things are a flowing,
> Sage Heraclitus says.[1]

When Abe sighed and sang his text at The Old Red Lion, we witnessed an act of what the American actor and director Joseph Chaikin called 'deep libidinal surrender,' a type of performance far removed from 'actioning' and all the other reductive 'methods' designed to suppress the unconscious and the metaphysical. The play, as it then was, demanded it and became active on a different plane. This has stayed with me and helped me to gain entry to this latest version, which is perhaps now more poem than play, but still holds the cry-the song-of that remarkable evening.

Rooney's writing is in a vein where as much is received as projected. He doesn't shout at you. He engages only with love, loss, death and the possibility of the infinite. The work is spiritually rather than socially active; the social referenced only as a vicious and unending tyranny, seen through a forest but with a tendency to come up close, founded on cruelty and injustice. His poem, its voices and its ghosts transmitted through the mind and body of a man living and suffering in the eye of the storm, at the very centre of life, seeks the sublime. The Pig Songs are the echo we crave, proof of our connectedness to a universe that exists beyond the fragile, disposable bodies, in which we can seem helplessly enclosed. They are the mark, the stain, the rhythm of our common blood, of family, of friends, of love. Through the songs, which seem to originate from the dead, the

---

1 Ezra Pound, *Hugh Selwyn Mauberley [Part I]*

dead and the living conjoin, and our brutal contemporary emphasis on the living only is relieved at last. It's no surprise that Rooney quotes from Bob Dylan's *Death Is Not The End* as the epigraph to the poem. I suspect he is a universalist as well as an essentialist. Each one of us will be saved, in whichever form. Earth and Heaven will see to it. But breathe, sing the songs.

> Wake me, shake me, free me from sin
> Make me invisible, like the wind.[1]

In the meantime, loss is the inescapable consequence of living. Ralph, Rooney's central man, is holed with it, made of it. His body is mostly sunk in a swamp, tethered only to a rope wrapped around a knife driven into the adjacent earth, in the midst of a war. This war, has claimed, he believes, the lives of his little boy Peter ('Peter is heaven') and the pregnant wife he adores, Lucy (Luce), both abducted by his foes. His enemies periodically throw apples in his direction, but not within his grasp. Ralph, however, leaves a space for hope. Like Walt Whitman in *Song of Myself*, 'he is waiting in gloom/Protected by frost.' But he is waiting. In this Hell, the Pig Songs are battle-cries, dream songs, love songs, death songs; how personal an affair is the war? He has killed members of the enemy force;

Luce, it's not easy
not when you see the enemy's lips trembling
dribble, saliva, blood.

---

1 Bob Dylan, *Mother of Muses*

Reality converts to dream. Over there? No, here. As long as the human (so often wicked, but sometimes saintly) is sustained, survival is possible. Ralph cries to his beloved Lucy:

You are the sea
You are the tides
You are the blood.

The poem flows from interior to exterior until the two become fused. The trees talk; 'They speak the Pig Songs/Ma always said.' The enclosed envelope of a human being opens and leaks pain. The immense hurt of Peter's loss runs along Ralph's spine. As David - Peter's godfather (a lovely man according to the near visionary Ma) and another of his ghost visitors, his arrival heralded by a spiderweb feeling over his cheeks and face - advises:

- Trauma sticks to your guts Ralph
- I hear you, David, I hear you
- You've got to let it out.

Ralph has been deprived of the actual tender feelings, the beauty of fatherhood, of touch. 'He knows before he can talk/ He knows me,' says a bewitched Ralph. But what remains? Death can't, mustn't be the end. Grace and resurrection are everywhere if you are open to receiving them. They take many forms, some almost imperceptible, others looming large:

Want a trail to the Pig Songs,
Peter can lead you there.

An I see us as a tribe,
Dancing on Peter's clouds.

*Pig Songs* is a life-fugue. Whatever dreams you set out with, whatever happiness you wring from life, you will be delivered to the swamp with many enemies circling (until they too lose interest and forget you) and a fractured tribe of loved ones, many dead - Ma, the kindly Pa, Luce, Peter, David, in Ralph's case. Some of us give up speaking to one another even while living; not even the note of a song heard.

While Ralph waits, the old red pram, intended to carry a blooming infant, is used by the enemy to serve as a coffin for the pregnant mother Lucy who they've raped, murdered, stitched up and left, like the apples, just out of Ralph's reach:

That's Lucy
Lying in the pram
It's her-dead-swollen body.

Black despair is the only possible response to those who would destroy the light and beauty in the universe. 'David's right, breath is the only honest thing there is.' (unless it's napalm). And it rhymes with death: breath and death. (The horse, briefly present, is movement and life, a creature of demonstrative breath). Ralph's desperate attempt to raise himself from the swamp, and join Lucy, using all his remaining strength, is resurrection and despair fused. Whoever survives and breathes will sing the songs of the living tribe and the dead. The narrow tribalism of the living only will be defeated. As Ma said; 'Breathe in the inspiration of the dead/Make them live again.' Ralph jumps into the pram, following Ma's instruction. We must learn not to fear the dead or even those parts of us which are dying daily. As Ralph demonstrates, this requires an animal strength and the lightness of an angel.

*Pig [Swamp] Songs*

★

# *The Tree Surgeon*

Easterly,
in the land of angles.

*You don't cut
them down
though
do you Ralph?*

*You
trim
them
back.*

These woods were once a wood without a name.

# *The Swamp [One]*

Ralph is sinking in a swamp.

He still has a few things with him.
For instance, a knife and a rope.
The knife is dug into the ground.
The rope is wrapped around.

It's holding him up a little.

Are you there, girl? Can you hear me? He calls.

There's very little light.
There is the sound of burning fires.
For now, they are far away.
But getting nearer.

There are many stories.
There are many voices.
There are many shadows.
There are many echoes.

There are spirits.
There are many spirits.

## *The Enemy's Apples [One]*

It makes Ralph freeze.
Apple after apple.
After apple, after apple.
A pause.

Then apple.
Then another.

Just the darkness, then.

# *The Swamp [Two]*

Ralph is grunting.
He's trying to lift himself,
Right out of the stink hole.
He knows time is passing.

Girl, are you there? Can you hear me?

There is a melody.
A choir, humming.
Surrounding him.
Replies to the Pig Songs.

*There are many spirits.*

You remember that story I used to tell?
I used to tell it to Peter, Ralph says.

Little fairies I'd call them.
Made from the stems of the leaves.
For wings they had those things
Which come from those flying seeds.

## *Interlude [One]*

It's snowing, or it could be falling leaves.
There is smoke drifting from the burning fires.

Ralph closes his eyes.

## *Leaf Fairies [One]*

Imagine a leaf in the autumn,
the stem all, brown an' red,
the thick bit at the end, its head.

Imagine a flying seed
The furry bits that come off
In the wind

Fly off in the sky
*That's what the wings are*
*That's what the wings are.*

When things get cold, you know what they do?

*Peter loves it, he loves this one so much.*

When things get cold.
Them little fairies
Wrap those leaves around themselves.

Like a little, what do we call them?
Just like one your Ma has
A poncho, a little poncho.

*Peter loves it, he loves this one so much.*

*He'd laugh.*
*He'd laugh.*
*Oh, he'd laugh, and he'd laugh.*

# *Leaf Fairies [Two]*

*Peter loves it, he loves this one so much.*

They play games Peter;
*Who's got the best poncho?*

Depending on the weather.

*Who's got the best poncho?*

This one's got the best poncho.
That one's got the best poncho.

They always have the best ponchos in Autumn.

All those colours.

## *Leaf Fairies [Three]*

*Oh, he'd laugh, and he'd laugh.*

Listen to me Peter.
You have to take care of yourself.
Look after what's in front of you.
Look after what's below you.

Then these fairies
They'll come to you
Fairies, spirits, gods.
All you gotta do.

All you gotta do,
Is sing
A Pig Song,
Or two.

★

## *Peter [One]*

Ralph moves his head.
He opens his eyes.
Looks around.
Nothing.

I'm waiting for 'em
Singing for 'em
And for you Peter, for your Ma.
They'll bring Ma back!

This plague will be over soon.
The fires will go out.

And we will sit at the table again.
You'll be there.
You won't be gone.
They won't have taken you.

You'll even have a sister.
A baby girl.
My Friend, uncle David, with his Cello
And we will break bread and we will sing songs!

Ralph breaks ever so slightly.

Your Ma is out there, Peter.
I know it.

Look at me, stuck in this place.

Enemy teasing me.

Can't reach these apples there they throw me.
You know me.
I'll make it.

Never give up.

Not when your Ma is out there- Lucy?



*Peter look, Luce…look at them…been torn a*

# *Lucy [One]*

Girl?

A moment.
I am still dreaming of him, even here.
That same one, same dream, again and again.

*Hell: fires burning.*
*Him, crawling.*
*Our bedroom walls moving in.*
*And I scream.*

Ma would call that just another,
different kind
of
Pig Song.

That these songs come in all different ways
not just on the wind or lakes but in dreams
and things too, that come from the other side.

That's what she'd say wouldn't she Lucy, girl?
If she were here.

Ma would say:

*Have no fear Ralph.*
*Have no fear Lucy.*
*Peter has left.*
*He's not gone.*

*It's Peter who sent that dream, that Pig Song.*

I hope she weren't wrong.
Luce, Luce, I miss you.
My thumbs hurt.

Ralph laughs.
Holds them up to the sky and out in front.


*part these hands from this war from this hole.*
                                                    Rests.

## *Pig Song [One]*

*I'm not lost*
*To the wind*
*No, I'm here*
*For it now.*

*And it hears*
*Me now:*
*I'm lost*
*To the ground.*

## *Interlude [Two]*

Passing of the night.
Into a new day.

Ralph is snoring, asleep on his arms,
He grips on to the rope wrapped around the knife.

## *The Enemy's Apples [Two]*

Another apple.

Ralph wakes.

Without moving a muscle, he watches.

Another apple.

Some time passes, he waits.

No more, no apples come.

# *The Swamp [Three]*

Ralph looks out and above, then all around.

Realising where he is.
He hangs his head.

They do talk to me. They do. They talk from the fields an' mountains.
They sing from there too.

David always said it is wise to listen
To the replies we get from our songs
If we listen
The answers come back.

Ralph listens.

Melodies
      Of
        Many
           Sung
              Replies

              From which, the voice of his Ma comes.

- It's all just a Pig Song Ralph.

My Ma would say.

## *Ma [One]*

                                            Cut from the same cloth,

- Such a lovely man, that David.
- He is.
- Such a lovely man.
- Yeh Ma.
- A lovely, lovely man.
  Plays the cello, doesn't he?
- He does.
- Incredible.
- What is?
- That he plays the cello. Doesn't look like he would, do he?
- Do I look like I cut down trees?
- You don't cut them down though do you Ralph, you trim them back.

And she's right. That's what I do.
Another voice breaks through.

# *David [One]*

Ma and David are.

- Sometimes Ralph.
  Sometimes if you can, after you've cut back those trees.
  Take a rest.
  Get still and have a sit down on the floor.
  Let your legs curl up.
  Let them cross.
  And sit still for a moment.
  Let yourself breathe with the floor.
  And the woods.
  Listen to them spirits speak.
  Focus on the centre of your head.
  The temple Ralph, right in the middle.
- David shut-

David touches Ralph's forehead.

- And let the light come in.
- Alright…
- Breathe it in.

Ralph breathes.

## *Spiderwebs*

Ma wasn't wrong cos I always shiver
Shudder
Goosepimples all over my skin whenever
I let them in.

What comes first, is the spiderweb feeling
Over my cheeks and my face.

Then, a light fizz on my ears, my neck,
The tingles.

And then, there they are:

## *Ma [Two]*

- They come from high Ralph

She was desperate,
Sat by the fire in our little room out back,
We had an old rocking chair then.
She'd rock with Peter and let him sleep.

This night she rocks alone.

I'm watching her from the doorway
Got the tingles
Rocking slows down
Fire is spitting.

*The sound of spitting fires.*

I know they're here.
They've come for her.
It's her turn.

And the tingles are all over me.
Hairs on end and I can barely stand.

So, I sing to them.
Help her pass along…

# *Pig Song [Two]*

*Send cover*
*Send rain*
*Send love*
*Send pain*

*Send mama*
*Send pa*
*Send short*
*Send far*

*Send sun*
*Send moon*
*Send hum*
*Send tune*

## *Interlude [Three]*

A melody swells. There is another voice. It's Ralph's Pa

- Are you cold?

Ralph shakes his head.

That's my Pa, Ralph says.

- You look cold Ralph.
  Look, go and grab the wood.
  That's it come on.
  Good lad, that's it…good boy…

He built that fireplace for you
And you rocked your way back to him
Rocking your spirit
Into the fire.

You went

## *Ma [Three]*

- We have to breathe with each other.

Ma would say.

Got to hear the others breathe
To know we are alive.

Ralph breathes in, coughs.
There is blood.
It's on his hands.

When he left, Ralph says.
Pa, he just collapsed backwards.
His body fell like a tree trunk.
And it don't mean nothing- it don't mean nothing.

- *Sing songs.*

Ma said.

- *Sing songs an' they come back*
  *Breathe air an' they come back*
  *Eat the foods an' sing the songs*

Ma said.

A melody swells.

## *Counting Trees [One]*

Ralph counts trees.

One. Two- six. Three. Four. Round! Again. One. Two. Six. Seven. No. Again. One. Two- six. Angel wings! Flies…an' that… Horses. Big, small ones. No. Yew. White Willow. Whitebeam. Crack Willow! One. Two. Black Poplar. Rowan. Horse, no mane…me here- Hornbeam. Holly New. Hazel tree- eyes… you have brown eyes – me hazel…One. Two. Hawthorn. Wych Elm. Wild Cherry. Silver Birch. Downy Birch. Aspen. Ash one, the favourite- like you…Alder tree…

He snores.

An apple is rolling towards.

In the darkness.

## *Interlude [Four]*

It seems to be snowing again, but it could be leaves falling.
A melody swells, black smoke.

Ralph is attempting,
Once more.
To lift himself
Out of the swamp.

I've been longing for it to snow or maybe rain.
Ralph says.
You know I feel the frost coming in
Towards.

Weather is changing.

Ralph catches a falling leaf.

All I'm getting are these falling leaves.

LEAVES!

Bloody petals.
    Leaves falling.
        the browns.
            the greens.
        and the brown–
        and the other one
    the red.

Sometimes I think they're snow.

BUT NO!

JUST BLOODY LEAVES!

Grunting, Ralph tries again to lift himself from the swamp.

Rests.

## *Lucy [Two]*

Luce?
Ralph calls.

Are you there?
Luce.

A melody swells, then disappears.
A swollen silence.

Luce my gums, they've been bleeding, coughing
up blood too my darling, my tongue is raw.
Fingernails are white and my eyes are burning.

Thought my body would- if I just think of
You, the light-
            breathe it in-

Sing a Pig Song or two.


I'd find my way back to you- not working.

- *Sing songs-*
  *Sing songs an' they come back*
  *Breathe air an' they come back*
  *Eat the foods an' sing the songs*


Maybe you come through the trees

Maybe
Maybe I catch a glimpse of you
From far off
Maybe I see something of you
Even before you appear

Maybe its light
Maybe
I can smell you

You're there an' you're light

And that's what keeps me–
our meals… mind racing…always…I'm getting tired….
mind racing.

## *David [Two]*

- Free yourself from the misery.
  Free yourself from the pain.
- Alright, David.

# *Lucy [Three]*

That's what these words are doing.
Our meals.
Remember the pork belly?
That belly always got the spot (in the gut) and fires me up.

My ribs are aching
But they're still willing.

My lungs are heavy
But they're still filling.

Remember
the rare beef, don't you girl?
Pickled sausages, fried potato
and lentil stew.

Ralph attempts to lift himself from the swamp.

Send me the light my darling
Send me a word or two.

Ralph falls.

That melody again.
Then the voice of an old man.

## *Old Man*

- What is it like to kill?

He asks me.

He's back in that town out there.

Through that forest there
that's where you'll come.

- Is it hard?

## *Lucy [Four]*

Luce it's not easy,
not when you see the enemy's lips trembling
Dribble, saliva, blood.

Mines
dripping
too.
From
his
body.

Through that forest there, is a town.

I spot them.

They've a woman-
treating her in ways I've never seen before.

- *Sing songs*
  *Sing songs an' they'll come back*
  *Breathe air an' they'll come back*
  *Eat the foods an' sing the songs.*


There's no Pig Song that can delete that stain
It stains my soul, what I see there.
She's on a chain,
They keep her watered and fed with a syringe.

Take it in turns to drip feed her.
Use her up.
    In all the ways.

## *The Enemy's Apples [Three]*

A rolling apple
        makes Ralph freeze.
He reaches for it.

        He does not
reach.

He waits.

Then bends over.
Leaning into the ground,
The melody somewhere swells.
So, he sings.

## *Pig Song [Three]*

*Will she be*
*Forgotten*
*Forbidden*
*Shunned, and all?*

*Will she be*
*Abandoned*
*Hidden*
*Lost to us all?*

## *Lucy [Five]*

Luce I'm sorry.
Ralph says.

Never told you what I see.
Worldliness.
You've got cunning.
You've strength.

I had to face that bloody murder
That forest
This void
This nothingness to realise.

Forgive me.
I love you so much I could eat you.

Explosions and fires crackling.

Do you hear that?

That melody swells and Ralph begins to cough.
Blood and all.

Rain.

Ralph opens his mouth.
He looks up.
Eyes closed.

I'm getting skin and bone my darling, losing fat.
Won't be much left.

Ralph drinks the rain.

That's like champagne my girl.

Luce. You see I sang a Pig Song for the rain and it came.

The wind and the rain won't desert me
Not while you're there.
It's on my side the weather is.
Frost coming in, the mist in the air crawls towards me.

Oncoming
Sticking to the air and then
Into my lungs.

It's still on my side see cos it's warmer now
This rain.

Pig Songs are answered.
Pig Songs are heard.

I wish I could see you smile Luce.
Hear you laugh.

So, somewhere Lucy laughs.
And Ralph closes his eyes.

*Can't even see your face.*

# *A Lake Memory*

You're dancing aren't you girl
In the sun
You, remember?

It was us
Just us – like when we first met.

We pack up, go and take off to the lake.

You're singing, dancing, playing
With nature.

There you are, twirling and swirling till
Your soul hits the light of the sun
You return back to where you come from.
You dig, without digging.
Fly without flying.
The way you beam. The way you.

*- Ralph?*


Lucy?

A moment.

That melody's back. Ralph shudders.

Seeing you be in the earth like that,
Bit like witnessing a great animal.

Watching you from the lake
As you dance on the bank
I'm treading water watching you
Battling against the sink and I'm just

Gawping.

## *Water*

*Tide like liquid…*
*Magic…*
*Power…*

Wish I'd sung a Pig Song for you
Or two,
Maybe two.

## *Lucy [Six]*

Are you still there, dancing girl?
Pulling the wind around you
At your whim.

Gliding through now you seem
Weightless, don't you?

Me, I can barely swim.

I witness you.
You, being you.

Natural, new again.
My soul sort of gets into my groin
r u m b l e s  f o r  y o u.

T
h
e
n

y
o
u

d
i
v
e

i
n

        Ah you're that very thing, aren't you?

## *Ma [Four]*

- She's precious…
- Yeh Ma.

## *Lucy Six [Reprise]*

You're the light aren't you Luce?

The beams go bouncing through your hair and it's
Like you're a spark of Pig Songs joined in dance
And love, and you're playing hide and
                                          seek.

                - You mustn't forget to remember.

*You are the sea*
*You are the tides*
*You are the blood.*
                        - Why do you love me?
Haven't got a choice.
It wasn't me who chose it.

The spiderwebs on my face. Tingles down my spine. Hair on end. Pimples all over. It's the Pig Songs that brought me you. The spirits hugged me the night before, and then you came. It was the Pig Songs.

   - *Sing songs*
     *Sing songs an' they come back*
     *Breathe air an' they come back*
     *Eat the foods an' sing the songs.*

# *Pig Song [Four]*

*Heaven*
*Or hell*
*Come back*
*My girl.*

*Winter*
*Or Spring*
*Summer*
*You bring.*

*Freedom*
*Or noose*
*Come back*
*My Luce.*

## *Interlude [Five]*

That melody swells.
Some sounds of war.
Spitting fires, inching nearer.

## *Lucy [Seven]*

Lucy here's what you have to do
Get through
the forest; come out the other side, you'll find me, I am sinking but when I see you I'll rise
like heavens breeze.

Come for me please.

## *The People's Soul*

The soul of our people is dirty.
What kings? Any, then heavy.
It's not just enemy
It's our friends that are burning.

Our children are being hurt.
I hear the beasts howling.

The night-time barely wants to come out
In fear of what its dark might do.

And so, I try and sing a Pig Song-

Ralph tries to sing-
He coughs up blood.

> - *Sing songs*
>     *Sing songs an' they come back*
>     *Breathe air an' they come back*
>     *Eat the foods an' sing the songs*

## *Lucy [Eight]*

Find it hard to feel you these, past few days
You know?

Ma said we should breathe with one another.
So, breathe.

Luce, breathe
        in these words.

Let your chest fill
        breathe the air between us.

If my  w o r d s  sail towards you
            swallow them.

Anchor them back to your skin,
            when you come

      through the forest bring
      the light that lights
      the words you sing.


You'll find me and I will lift myself free
From this stink
        tell you all about it, every bit.


We will talk of Peter.

David.
Ma.
Pa.
and our little girl will be born.

We can play in the garden,
sit in the playroom
w o o d e n  t o y s.

Make a fire in the pit, heat these memories into good ones.

Luce find me, find me Luce.

## *Interlude [Six]*

Ralph coughs.
The crackling fires are getting closer.

Then rain, falls heavy.

Ralph waits.
Hears the bird song.

## *The Rain*

That rain
is running
down
my spine.

I can see you now that my back is straight
I can feel you.

I'm brushing your hair.
You silent, on my knees.

There we are two apes grooming,
reaching for the Pig Songs.

Spirits above this plain.

Thunder and lightning then, that melody swells.

## *The Enemy's Apples [Four]*

Another apple.
Ralph freezes, and waits,
another.

Attempts a lunge for one.
Can't
      reach.

Goes for the sky instead.

Fires crackling, getting louder, that melody swells again.

## *Bird Song*

I see black birds
                blue, red ones
perching on the heads of the dead bodies
that hang from the trees.

The weight of them pulling down the branches
closer to the water, I can just see
                              the tufts of their
hair
catching the light, reflecting off the surface.


Want these dead bodies to be birds, my heart wants
them to be birds

but they're heads, and the lake is turning red.
Heads tipping over and then dripping blood


                              I think of us swimming
                                      in that lake
                                    I swear I see
                                        the light

                s h i m m e r   t h r o u g h.


                                              I

                                    s
                                    w
                                    e
                                    a
                                    r

                                    I

                                    d
                                    o

I feel it in my temples,
and if blood can vibrate then it makes
a dreary sound in me.

# *Pig Song [Five]*

*Them we be there for me
angels sing there for me
Their bodies are free
and our songs, high!*

*Them we be there for me
angels sing there for me
Their bodies are free
and our songs, high!*

## *Lucy [Nine]*

Ralph pushes himself up.
It's cold. He says.

There I am. There you are.
Wrapped once more like apes, in our cold and wet.

You remember that girl?

Our room, damp, full of grey, you're fidgeting
I'm watching you in that half-light.

I see how you are alive, and I do
Wonder if Peter is there with you, in your dark
With you
In your dream.

# *David [Three]*

- The brain is like a machine
- Alright David
- At night it processes all the thoughts from that day.
- Okay, go on then David.
- Swirls them around into ones you understand.
  And ones you don't.
- Right.
- Anything not understood gets stuck in the body.
- In the muscles!
- That's right.
  Trauma gets stuck to you like glue.

- What a lovely man. Ma would say.

*Maybe Peter was with you in your dream Luce.*

- Trauma sticks to our guts Ralph.
- I hear you David, I hear you.
- You've got to let it out.

David is there after Peter leaves.
Isn't he Luce?

Sits there, shining.
His little grin.
Tears in his eyes, smiling
Like he's taking the pain from us.
I swear those tears were Peter's from beyond.

## *You Trim Them Back*

When I trim those trees
I'm in and around them
And I can hear them talk
To one another.

They speak the Pig Songs.
Ma always said
They come in on the wind
You've got to listen.

I swear Luce I hear them.
I close
        my eyes and I just
let them take me.

Ralph closes his eyes.

My neck goes.
                My shoulders
                              dip.
Ma used to say *angels dance on tip toes.*

# *Ma [Five]*

- If Pa visits me now
- You get shivers, don't you ma?
- I do, and spiderwebs on my face.
- Breathe inspiration.
- That's it.

*Breathe air and they come back.*

Ralph lifts up his arms like angels' wings.

- Listen and you'll hear little crackling noises.
- Yeh, I can hear them Ma.
- Listen to them.
- No, I hear, I do hear them.
- They're the replies to our Pig Songs.

Ralph takes   a   l o n g   breath, then lets his head

drop.

- I can feel it Ma,
- Yes, see that's it.
- Eh. It's tingling.
- That tingling is ours, and theirs.
- And mine, and yours?
- Yes.

Ralph shivers and then shudders, arms like wings.
With closed eyes, he reaches high

for the skies.

## *Interlude [Seven]*

I can see angels on tiptoes, eh boy,
I'm coming for you Peter, you hear, boy?
My friend, David.
Ma.
Pa.
No, I'm here.

You hear me?
I have to keep on living.
Of course, I want to be with ya.

Of course, I miss ya.
But this body's still on the ground
Aching; you'd feel the same
We're no different.

You're just there, and I'm just here, see.


It begins then to snow, or is it leaves?

## *Pig Song [Six]*

*Oh, my brother, my brother oh.*
*Help me my brother, my brother oh.*

*This ain't easy, this ain't sweet*
*This ain't easy, this ain't sweet*
*Wishing now, you would help me*
*Help me to see*

*Oh, brother help me, help me to see*
*Help me my brother, help me to be.*

*Oh, my brother, my brother oh.*
*Help me my brother, my brother oh.*

## *The Enemy's Apples [Five]*

There is then another apple.
There is then a new kind of silence.
Ralph, staring
         at the apple, staring
at the silence.

# *The Famous [Red]*

From the silence comes
                    a Man in the famous red.

Nothing for ya, Ralph says.
Sinking..

The man takes out a knife, holds it in front of him.

                         *Tie blow de co. Ta blah fee fee.*

I don't speak.

        T h e   m a n  b e l l o w s

He goes to the ground. Crosses his legs, takes a pouch of tobacco and rolls one. Rolls another. Then slowly crawls to Ralph, and puts one in his mouth, for him. Then lights them. They sit.


    R a l p h  n o d s  h i s  h e a d  f o r  s o m e  t i m e

Thank you, Ralph says.
Can't help me.

Know any Pig Songs?

No trouble.

*Te ass colo lolo*
*Sen be la te dro dro*
*Les dem be go fo fo*

*fo-*

*Les dem-*

*oh- les dem…*

*be go fo fo!*

*fo, fo!*

*Te ass colo lolo*
*Sen be la te dro dro*
*Les dem be go fo fo*

*Les dem be go fo fo*          *Les dem be go fo fo*

t h e y  n o d  together.

The man crawls to Ralph and whispers to him. Places a hand on his forehead for a moment, leaves.

Another apple.

Ralph stares at the apple,
            and then he sings:

*Les dem be go fo fo*
*Les dem be go fo fo*

- *Sing songs*
  *Sing songs an' they come back*
  *Breathe air an' they come back*
  *Eat the foods an' sing the songs.*

That's what Ma said.
Must be true.

# *David [Four]*

- Dreams enter the brain from the body
- Oh David!
- Up through the spine Ralph.
- David-
- When the days gone, thoughts disappear.
- Do we have to do this now David?
- No more words to put to the things we see out in front of us.
- Okay. Okay. Slow down David.
  You mean when we see things,
  we put words to them.
- Yes.
- Yeah. Got that bit…then you mean at night, we just see darkness, for a moment.
- That's it.
- Then what, David?
- Well then, your memories…
  traumas come from the body,
  up the spine and into your brain.
  To fill the darkness.
- Sorry David…okay so the eyes are shut,
  no labelling, no naming trees or anything,
  just dark.
- That's it, Ralph.
- Got that bit.
- Good, so, Ralph, we are so backlogged with-
- Yup.
- Misunderstood concepts.
- Right…right David… wait a second…okay…

## *Interlude [Eight]*

I'm carrying some cuttings, plenty of fog
Can barely see in front of me, can hear
Birds rustling, blue ones, black an' red no doubt.

- What if there were no labels or concepts.
- Ah, what if?
- Oh…right…yes!
- So, the spine Ralph, it lifts the thoughts,
  the memories into the brain,
  the forgotten bits
  and makes up the images of our dreams.
- Yeah that makes sense…
- Does doesn't it? Does make sense.
  Listen to your dreams.
  They are speaking your fears to you–

Desires, loves, cuts an' wounds
                                        that's what he says.
Ralph coughs, inspects his
                                        phlegm and blood.
He says that it all comes
                                        out from our gut
In phlegm and blood,
                                        he's not wrong is he, eh?

- So, go on David.
- Dreams are your soul's way of speaking to you.
  The bits of your soul that stick to your
  skin, bones and flesh.
- Ok, so, my soul is trying to–
  I don't know, get rid of 'em?
- Transform them, when you're still and silent, facing
  the darkness behind your eyes.
- No, I don't understand it David.
  I'm trying to, I'm listening, but you do keep

- speaking in riddles.
- All I am saying, is when you sleep you start for a moment, empty.
- No, I get that.
- You are aware that you are not aware.
- I don't get that bit
- Fear, longing, let it all go, let your heart sing.
- Pig Songs?
- They will reach up high if you want them too.

## *Ma [Six]*

Ma said just
breathe in the inspiration of the dead
make them live again
an' you'll hear

those crackling sounds
the gods are taught are theirs

## *Interlude [Nine]*

I'm carrying cuttings, its dark
Not much sight
         I can see birds
and my favourite tree.

And there he is: David.
He's watching me. Now he's barely there,
                            But he is there, He's
made up of fog an' rain an' I can
feel
the spiderwebs tingle across my face, an' he's coming from
the other side, his soul just inching in.
                            Him, almost there,
almost touching skin, barely he was, but I knew.

## *Ma [Seven]*

- You'll get tingles down your spine Ralph
- Whenever Pa comes?
- Tingles down your spine.
  Feelings of spiderwebs on your face.

*That's what I get when I see David*

## *David [Five]*

He stands there
An' he's playing some cello song

A gentle one, something mellow, a forgotten one.

I wish I could see now,
Wish I could hear him now.

> *Eh David, if you're there*
> *I can only hope for this*
> *For a song*
> *A little song*
>
> *.*

## *Lighter Now, Riding Clouds [One]*

When Peter is born
He has this way of looking which seems like
He's somewhere on a cloud
An' David knows it.

I mean he doesn't know
He just has a feeling, I suppose.

David plays these songs he has
And they ride an' rumble past me
An' sink into me
They skip off me an' over you.

And I'd imagine us in fields as a family
Then as a couple
And then just me.

## *Lighter Now, Riding Clouds [Two]*

Then it's us again
An' maybe a friend of the furry kind
A dog maybe
Or something more exotic, who knows?

I might like a horse sometime.

## *Lighter Now, Riding Clouds [Three]*

And then I see you go dancing in your layered skirts
With their dreamy holes in
With the white flashing out
The brown of your skin
                        And the touch of your hand
So like a deep breath in

An' his face, little Peter, he's not bigger than a baby
Yet here now in my mind to cello he dances
Like a little orange dragon lost from his crew
Not in a bad way mind, but in a good way.

## *Lighter Now, Riding Clouds [Four]*

And we dance, my hands high
I reach for something up there, something which
from here feels like the sky
but with my tiptoes raised
                        my heart out
                                              and my mind at rest well
this sky is water for my leathery soul.

## *Lighter Now, Riding Clouds [Five]*

When he walks
That time, the first time
He giggles every step
And David plays a march to every giggle.

An' they ride an' rumble like waves in the sky
They lead me to clouds which
David's cello draws for me in my mind
Dancing tide of touches without touches

Oh, that gentle carefree caress
An' like those simple marches, he plays.

## *Lighter Now, Riding Clouds [Six]*

Peter marches like a solider on the spot
Stamps for joy
Baby dancing to the beat of a giggle an'
A crescendo of cello strings from afar

-barely there-

Only in my mind now and yet its fire and water and dust.
Earth, it's Earth's rumble
How Peter rumbled.

Raucous, full.
He walks like he'll never fall.

# *Peter [One]*

- *Sing songs an' they come back*
  *Breathe air an' they come back*
  *Eat the foods and sing the songs*

Eh Peter I'm here. Ralph says.
Daddy is here and I'm not going anywhere.

## *Interlude [Ten]*

Ralph attempts to lift himself from the swamp.
He cries and curses but tries some more.
Then gives up, pants and rests for a moment.
Coughs up blood, inspects it
                             starts counting trees.

# *Counting Trees [Two]*

Hornbeam and Holly…Hazel…you've got brown eyes– me hazel. Hawthorn…Wych Elm…Wild Cherry at the helm… Silver Birch…you have brown eyes…Downy Birch…brown and Beach and Aspen…Ash one too, that's my favourite one…

# *The Enemy's Apples [Six]*

Another apple comes.
Ralph stares it down.

## *Peter's Twin*

There's this boy in that town back there
Through the forest
He's got this frown for a smile

It's this plague that gave him that frown no doubt.
He's like Peter, I think.

So, then Peter comes flying into mind
Peter Pan I used to call him
Flying around like a little lost boy,
                              no shadow
He was light

But this boy has dark eyes
If Peter is heaven
This boy is something else.

## *Worth It*

It hard, pushing him out?
That flesh and bone, cos Luce
*If it were, if it were*
*Were worth it,* weren't it?

## *Gentle Forehead*

I can see him now
His gentle forehead
His tiny elbows
The way he would stand

Me laying down
His eyes are on me
He knows, before he can talk
He knows me

Better than I know myself.

## *David [Six]*

- He's not forgotten to remember.
- David, he's just beautiful
- When he's looking at you like that Ralph
- What, David?
- Well look.
- Yeh, he knows me.
- He does.
- Yeh, what else David?
- What else is there Ralph?

## *Pebble Eyes [One]*

He sings the Pig Songs with his eyes, my boy.
Ralph tries to lift himself up, coughs, then rests.

Like pebbles his eyes;
They see my soul, make me see his.

His eyes, are so fresh
They can see past these lines an' pain     and in through my
dazzlers         to my brain
down my spine into the guts of me.

## *David [Seven]*

- Let him guide you
- I don't know David
- I'm not asking you to know
- David you're always theorising…waxing lyrical
- Am I?
- Aren't you? Where's your baby David?



- I'm sorry.



- Want a true trail to the Pig Songs?
  Peter can lead you there.

## *Pebble Eyes [Two]*

Looking into his eyes
                  It's like traveling through all of time. You
know sometimes it's like he's leading me deeper into you.
An' I see us as a tribe
            dancing on Peter's clouds.

## *David [Nine]*

- What if I don't want the Pig Songs?
- Then the Pig Songs will come anyway.
- I don't want them David.
- They want you.


Ralph almost breaks.

## *Lucy [Ten]*

When Peter goes you grip on to me
Don't you babe, Luce, don't ya?

Ralph whimpers like an ape.

You're all curly and floppy.
All soft in my arms and we're apes again.

Whimpers.

No focus, no thought.

## *David [Nine]*

- Suffering is your gateway
- I don't want to suffer
- You will suffer.
- I don't want to David.
- You already have Ralph, haven't you?
- I suppose.
- Open to it. Let it set you on fire.
- They've taken him
- No. You took him.

## *Masses of Blood*

We're just masses of blood mixed with salt
                                  pain sticking to us.
That's what I am now
                    just salt and blood.

That's all I am.

## *David [Ten]*

- I am just bones David.
- If you believe that why do you keep singing?
- No choice.
- Why?
- Hurts not to.


- Not to what Ralph?
- To reach.
- For what?
- Sky, or something.

## *Lucy [Eleven]*

You push your head so hard into me that it's soft.
Ralph brings his chest to the floor, on the edges.

He knew. Peter knew, Luce, he knew.

Somehow him leaving
               he left us this, this closeness, this dark.

# *David [Eleven]*

- Face the dark every day.
- I don't want it.
- When you do, you'll see it all as new.
- I don't want it.
- All of it, new again.
- No, I wanna leave.
- The trees you trim will speak to you.
- David stop please-
- Ralph look at me. I love you.
  We are best friends. You've been there for me.
  And I am here for you.
- Yeh I know.
- I am not telling you what's easy.
  I am telling you what is true.

# *Lucy [Twelve]*

Ah it's all so timeless isn't it.
Our flesh is dancing somehow
We're, I don't know, shuddering.
But we are silent, and we are still.

# *David [Twelve]*

- Ah…it hurts.
- Just sit with it
- Ah! It hurts David.
- Sit into it.
- Ah fuck I hate it.
- Let it be there.
- Okay.
- Lucy is true.
- David I can't do this.
- She will love you.
- Yeh I love her.
- Be with her.
- Uhuh.
- Hold her. Peter knows.

# *Lucy [Thirteen]*

I think he watches
He would wouldn't he
He'd watch
      from beyond he'd watch


                      probably watching now in't ya
Peter.

Luce, are you?
      In some tent.
         In some tent in some field in some, in some
field, if they have you, if they've got you.

      In some tent in some field full of rot
                      Stay alive girl.
Stay alive.

Do you hear me?
Peter is watching us.
David too.
Ma and Pa.

They're not ready for us.

Not yet.

## *Interlude [Eleven]*

Ralph gives into the ground.
Coughs a few times. More blood.

That melody swells.
He attempts to lift himself from the swamp.

Screams in agony.
Attempts a few more lifts.

Gives up.
Pants.

Rests for a moment.

# *The Enemy's Apples [Seven]*

Another apple.
Ralph stares at the apple,
                starts counting trees.

# *Counting Trees [Three]*

Hornbeam…Holly …Hazel eyes- you have brown eyes…
Wild Cherry at the helm…Silver Birch…Downy Birch and
Beach and Aspen…favourite one is…alder tree-

I've seen death before
And I can see it again

Luce…
Those hanging bodies
They do
They look like birds but…they're not birds.

I've seen death before
And I can see death again.

Hornbeam and Holly…Hazel Tree- You've got brown eyes.

- *Sing songs and they come back-*

## *Interlude [Twelve]*

No!
No watery eyes no stinging sights no filthy stench no dripping guts no heads in lakes no toes cut off no fingers loose or marrow brown- no shit in my mouth or wax in my ears-

- *Breath the air and they come back-*

Tired bones.
Ah I've seen death before.

*A distant sound of war.*
*Then that melody swells.*

# *The Horse [One]*

I can see this horse
                I could be dreaming
But there's a horse
                I'm barely sleeping here

She comes from afar
        an' she's in the distance
                              an' there's this stream in me
                              which is desperate to fall out.

# *The Only Honest Thing [One]*

- We have to breathe with one another.
- That's what David says Ma.
- David's right, breath is the only honest thing there is.

## *The Horse [Two]*

This horse breathes so easy Luce
A beast at ease with herself
An' I want to breathe as I watch her
But my heart is afraid.

She's so gentle, and my heart's vicious.
My heart's hardened. My heart is weary.

She's coming towards me.

# *The Only Honest Thing [Two]*

- When we breathe
  We breathe the air in this world, and the next.
- Pa is waiting for you Ma.
- He's laid the path with breath.

## *The Horse [Three]*

Ralph gulps in air.

It's cold and damp,
The air we share knows the deepest parts of me

Gulps again.

She comes closer to me
She's warm and that
                           spills through me
Gulps again.

She neigh, neigh, neighs me.

Knows I'm stuck,
        She knows I'm sinking.

Neigh, neigh, neighs me.

Brushes me with her head.

She neigh, neigh, neighs me.

She's got her head near me,
She's trying to help me out.

Ralph attempts to lift himself.

Neigh, neigh, neighs me.

# *The Enemy's Apples [Eight]*

Another apple. Ralph stares.

## *Counting Trees [Four]*

You…white willow whitebeam crack willow…I've seen dreams of trees on fire… horse instead of you…Hornbeam and Holly-Hazel tree hazel eyes…you had brown eyes. Brown ones.

That melody swells.

## *An Old-Fashioned Pram [One]*

The enemy are inching closer
Pushing an empty
Old-fashioned pram.

The famous red
Pushes the pram, rolls apples
Towards Ralph.

Ralph watches.

Stares.

Apples.

> - *Eat the foods and sing the*

*pram is gone.*

# *Pig Song [Eight]*

*Seen the sky filled*
*With red and blue*
*Seen these lilies*
*Shine for you.*

*Seen the sky filled*
*With red and blue*
*Seen these lilies*
*Shine for you.*

## *Pa [Two]*

- Ralph you got to learn to look after *you*.
- Yes Pa.

- *Sing songs an' they come back*
  *Breathe air an' they come back*
  *eat the foods an' sing the songs*


*Seen the sky filled*
*With red and blue*
*Seen the lilies*
*Shine for you.*

Ralph manages to get an apple.
                            He takes a bite.
                                                  Chews.

Ralph finishes the apple, throws the core to one side.

## *Luce*

Ah!

We are going to dance Luce!
We are going to dance on clouds!
In fields of lilac
an' daffodils an' lavender!

## *Tapestry*

When I name those trees
Peter's there, Luce
He's with me
An' I hear David play his cello

Ma,
on her rocking chair
Facing Pa
as the fire of the home.

Ah!

I miss whisky
want some wine
that's when, ya know
I get warmer below

We're naked an' you're soft.
I dreamt of a horse, but I think it was you.

# *David [Thirteen]*

- If she left what would you do?
- Why are you asking me these things David?
- Who would you be?
- I don't understand what you're asking…?
- I'm asking you, if she is taken away, what would you do?
- I don't know!
  I'd cry David
- You do know, what would you do?
- I'd look at the stars.
  I love doing that.
- What do you see?
- Death.
  Like I'm just living to prepare for that.
  For them.

# *Lucy [Fourteen]*

When we met

I never told you this
I never said

But I go down to that little shanty by the sea

with that old deck chair of mine
I take it an' I settle myself down

I've got my tobacco
an' some rum

*Cheers rum!*
*Cheers tobacco!*

# *David [Fifteen]*

- What did they tell you Ralph?
- They said she's mine an' I am hers.
- And do you believe them?
- I don't know.
- If she left. If they take her away.
  Are you still hers?
- I don't know.
  Don't really understand what you're asking me.

## *Interlude [Thirteen]*

Can't the wind tell me
Been singing the songs
Maybe if the snow came
The fires would burn out.

Leaves fall like snow.

Ma, I am
I am singing the songs.

Ma,
I'm singing, Pa.

Peter.

Fires burn.
Leaves fall.

## *Large Bump*

When you were in your Mummy's
tum
You were a large
bump.

## *Where'd He Come From*

- Where did he come from?
- Well, I put him there didn't I?
- Did you?
- Yes.

## *Reasons*

                          Luce, I know you've been
                                        searching
                                              for

                                reasons.

       *Why did they take him?*

                                                       I
                                            don't
                                            know.

               *I wish I did*
               *I wish I knew*
                 *I wish*

                   *I want*
                     *to*
                   *fix it.*

                                          *But*
                                          *I*
                                     *can't.*

# *David [Sixteen]*

- Where do we come from and where are we going?
- Look David can we-
- Where did Peter come from?

*That melody swells.*

Ma just said sing the songs and they'll come back, breathe the air- they'll come back, eat the food an' sing the songs…

## *Peter [Two]*

Peter when you were small
        when you were small
when you were born
        you were so small when

you were born.

Sometimes I see birds in the trees
An' they are as small as you were then.

Pa used to put me on his knees
An' rock me like I was on a horse
It's all of us
That's what Ma would say.

When she rocked you on her lap
                facing the fire which kept his
                      spirit burning
There was a Pig Song
or two.

I am all those things
I am all that time.

# *The Enemy's Apples [Nine]*

Another apple.

## *Remembering Trees*

When I trim those trees
                      sometimes

Sometimes apples fall
from them

        some are bruised and brown
some are red
                and juicy

but mostly they are green and bitter
I can't eat 'em
                I can just stare at them.

                                              Leaves fall
                                  Ralph watches them fall.

Ma would call this just another,
Different kind of Pig Song.
They come in all different ways
On the wind, on lakes, and in dreams and things too,
                        that come from the other side.
                        That melody swells, more leaves.

I wish my body would burn
I wish I could be lost to the wind
                                    Like the leaves.
                                        I wish
                              I could be with them.

  Too

                                        Peter
                                        Ma
                                        and
                                        Pa

                                        And
                                        David

Luce, where are you?

# *Interlude [Fourteen]*

My eyes are heavy

                                                                                                 He coughs blood


                              I can hear footprints

I can do it

                      Look them right in the face

                                                      I can kill them

                                                         I am nothing

                        I am pointless

I blame

                        I blame

                                                     I wish I knew

                              I don't even know my own name.

## *A Tap*

There is a tap that floats                       in the high sky Peter,
it's letting water stream down

                                      and I saw
                                   that in a dream
                               that came from the
                                   Pig Songs


              that came from the spirits.


Two days later
Your Ma is pregnant.

        *It will be a girl,* she says.

                You'd have a baby sister Peter
                     If your Ma is out there

                 If you can hear me Peter
                            Go to her.

                                Look.
                 Show her you're there.

                             Tell her
                           I am here.

                 Lead her to me,

                        that tap, that tap is dripping water
                                        that water is my sweat
                                            my spittle
                                            my blood

that water is my blood

            an' my sweat an'

                    my spittle

                            maybe I have

                                    a daughter.

## *Interlude [Fifteen]*

That melody swells.
Brings a few more apples.

Ralph tries to sing,
                but can't.


                                      He coughs more blood.

*Peter*
*When you were gone*
*Ah*
*She sunk*
*She got so blue.*

## *David [Seventeen]*

- I don't know what to do David.
- Just be there.
- No, I want to fix it.
- You can't.
- Don't tell me that.
- There's nothing to fix.
- I want her to get better.
- Then what? It's not gonna get better Ralph.
- Then what's the point?

      I tried Peter
    to get to the bottom
      …deep…blue….

- You can't save her Ralph.
- I love her.
- Then love her.
- I want it gone-
- Let her be.

    …I'm holding her…
…night after night I'm holding her…
     …we're making love…
…I barely remember the place in my brain…
  …but we go there every single night….
     …and we come together…
    …*you* brought us together…

- That feels strange David.
- What does?
- Feels like we're closer cos of him.
- You're loving her.
- Am I?
- You're remembering not to forget.
- What, Peter?
- Maybe.
  But other things too.
- He knew.
  My sweet boy, he knew.


>   Thank you, Peter –
>   for bringing me my wife back.

## *That Night*

Peter when they came,
      they came in the night,

They came with their fire an' guns
                they came with their blood and spittle

      and Ma and Me
we're making love like the Pig Songs are calling us

           an' we're skin
         dust on dust

                    they bang down the doors
                      already had you

      and now they want her.

# *The Enemy's Apples [Ten]*

Another apple.
        Another leaf falls.
Ralph stares.

That's when I go to war.
                No Choice.

## *Lady in the City [One]*

Luce, we made it to the city not far from here
Just through that forest there
They've got a lady tied up
She's in chains and stuff.

They're watering her with syringes.
I told ya
They use her up
In all the ways I reckon.

# *The Old-Fashioned Pram [Reprise]*

The enemy is there again,
with that same old-fashioned pram.

That's Lucy,
lying in the pram
it's her dead -swollen- body.
Apples falling from the pram.

## *Lady in the City [Two]*

I sing a Pig Song
or two.

But nah
Nothing rids you of that

They stitched her up
Nothing getting in
 nor out,
 not anymore.

## *Interlude [Sixteen]*

The enemy pushes the pram
Rings its old bell

*tring*

                      *tring*

                                          *tring*

                             Ralph watches.

                      Follows them as they move
                                apples are
      falling from everywhere
        the enemy stops
        places the pram


        two metres or so
          from him
      out of    reach

        then leaves.

Ralph freezes.
        He stares.

                                    Leaves fall.

## *Counting Trees [Five]*

Hornbeam Holly new…hazel-brown eyes…me hazel, you've got brown.

That melody swells.

## *Slow March*

Ralph pulls himself from the swamp.
Then falls.

    His hand reaching for the pram
                      for his wife.

He's lying
        on his face.

A little time passes.

    He crawls then, towards her,

            makes it to her.

                Uses her body to pull
                          his up.

                    *Ah, she's cold.*

                Ralph falls to his knees
                    Closes his eyes

                  The melody swerves
                  As more leaves fall

Ralph takes Lucy from the pram
                               down to the floor
                                    her in his arms
                                   takes her hand
                              and begins
                             to pull her along
                      the floor back
               towards the swamp
        there is some light breaking
through
      his body looms in shadow
he looks to the sun.
                   Slow march to the stink hole
                              more lightbreaksthrough
                               places his dead wife inside the
hole.

Looks up and sings:

- *Send cover, send rain*
  *Send love, send pain*

                                           Leaves falling.
                                             Not snow.

★

ralph stands with hands in prayer
above his head

then
he
jumps
in.

*The Pig Songs*

# *Pig Song [One]*

*I'm not lost*
*To the wind*
*No, I'm here*
*For it now.*

*And it hears*
*Me now:*
*I'm lost*
*To the ground.*

# *Pig Song [Two]*

*Send cover*
*Send rain*
*Send love*
*Send pain*

*Send mama*
*Send pa*
*Send short*
*Send far*

*Send sun*
*Send moon*
*Send hum*
*Send tune*

# *Pig Song [Three]*

*Will she be*
*Forgotten*
*Forbidden*
*Shunned, and all?*

*Will she be*
*Abandoned*
*Hidden*
*Lost to us all?*

## *Pig Song [Four]*

*Heaven*
*Or hell*
*Come back*
*My girl.*

*Winter*
*Or Spring*
*Summer*
*You bring.*

*Heaven*
*Or hell*
*Come back*
*My girl.*

## *Pig Song [Five]*

*Them we be there for me
angels sing there for me
Their bodies are free
and our songs high!*

*Them we be there for me
angels sing there for me
Their bodies are free
and our songs high!*

# *Pig Song [Six]*

*Oh, my brother, my brother oh.*
*Help me my brother, my brother oh.*

*This isn't easy, this isn't sweet*
*This isn't easy, this isn't sweet*
*Wishing now, you would help me*
*Help me to see*

*Oh, brother help me, help me to see*
*Help me my brother, help me to be.*

*Oh, my brother, my brother oh.*
*Help me my brother, my brother oh.*

## *Enemy Pig Song*

*Te ass colo lolo*
*Sen be la te dro*
*Les dem be go fo fo*
*Les dem be go fo fo*

*Te ass colo lolo*
*Sen be la te dro*
*Les dem be go fo fo*
*Les dem be go fo fo*

## *Pig Song [Seven]*

*Seen the sky filled*
*With red and blue*
*Seen these lilies*
*Shine for you.*

*Seen the sky filled*
*With red and blue*
*Seen these lilies*
*Shine for you.*